Past and Present

Every season brings its own brand of magic to Pen Llŷn, including those rare winter occasions when the hills are shrouded in snow. But it's hard to beat the summer view from Mynytho or Llanbedrog when the heather is in bloom and the sea in Abersoch at its deepest blue. It's worth taking a few minutes to climb to the summit of Foel Gron (*Moel* = hill, *cron* = round) or Mynydd Tir y Cwmwd (*Mynydd* = mountain, *tir* = land, *cwmwd* = commote) and look towards Ynysoedd Tudwal (*ynysoedd* = islands), over Bae Ceredigion and as far as the Mynyddoedd Preseli on a clear day. The coastal foreground between Mynydd Rhiw and Llanbedrog is the subject of this little book. No-one could dispute its designation as an area of outstanding natural beauty.

At its centre is Abersoch, a tourist attraction sometimes advertised as the Welsh Riviera. The area, or *ardal*, has been welcoming strangers for centuries before bed and breakfast became an industry. These visitors – saints and pilgrims, sailors and miners – were absorbed into the *Cymreictod* (Welshness) of the comminity and left their marks and their names on villages, coves and churches. Present day visitors who become acquainted with this heritage can take something home more lasting than their suntan to remind them of the *ardal*.

Abersoch from Mynydd Tir y Cwmwd

Beckham and March Amheirchion

Abersoch harbour

David and Victoria Beckham were buying a house in Abersoch. Local people knew which house, and one or two had discussed the matter with Becks himself over a pint in the White House Hotel. The story inspired ac anti-second homes protest by *Cymdeithas yr Iaith Gymraeg* (Welsh Language Society). But to the disappointment of Manchester United and Spice Girl fans, and the relief of others, the story wasn't true: it was simply a rural version of an urban legend.

If it's hard to distinguish between fact and fiction in present day matters, what hope is there when the alleged events happened thousands of years ago? Beyond Ynysoedd Tudwal, the reef known as Sarn Badrig or Saint Patrick's Causeway extends from the Harlech area towards Ynys Enlli, or Bardsey Island. According to legend it was one of the embankments of Cantre'r Gwaelod, a fertile and magical place submerged when drunken watchman Seithennyn left the floodgate open. The earliest record of the story is in a poem in Llyfr Du Caerfyrddin, the oldest surviving Welsh manuscript, dating from 1250. But did it stem from the poet's imagination, or from the folk memory of a previous tragedy? Tree trunks appear in Bae Ceredigion at low tide, and it's known that *Cymru* and Ireland were joined by land been before the end of the Ice Age, around 7,000 BC. Was that land submerged gradually, or was there some catastrophic event that might be known today as a tsunami? Whatever the truth, some romantics still listen for the church bells of Cantre'r Gwaelod ringing beneath the sea.

Fairies were among the early visitors to

Sarn Badrig

Rushes on the banks of Afon Soch

Abersoch. They would arrive on their little white horses and ask the lady who lived in the mill, Felin Soch, if they could borrow a pan to bake bread. They would show their gratitude by leaving her a little white loaf before riding away again. Some people can still see the fairy rings near the old mill above the village.

Opposite the entrance to the huge Warren holiday park is the location of one of Cymru's best-known legends. Castellmarch is now a farmhouse, but according to tradition it was once the site of a castle occupied by March Amheirchion, one of King Arthur's knights. March had a secret which he was determined to conceal from the world: he was born with a horse's ears. So he kept his hair long, and on the rare occasion when he had a haircut the servant assigned the task would thereafter disappear. But the secret came out when a musician who had been summoned to play at a banquet in the castle went to a nearby bog to gather reeds for his flute. What the guests heard, instead of music, was a loud whisper declaring that March had a horse's ears. One of the murdered ex-barbers had been buried among the reeds.

We'll return to Castellmarch in other chapters, but one question remains: if David Beckham had indeed moved to Abersoch, who would been assigned to cut his hair and keep his secrets?

Castellmarch

Forts

The panoramic view over land and sea is not the only reason for climbing Pen-y-gaer, overlooking the road from Abersoch to Llanengan. The site itself has the remains of an oval-shaped hill fort from the Iron Age. Much of it has been destroyed by agriculture, mining and the quest for building stones, but you can still try and envisage the lives of the generations who lived here in the last centuries BC. Within two defensive walls there are hollows where two round stone huts would have stood. It must have been in a good position to defend, but the surrounding walls were not high and the residents may not have been in any great danger form invaders. They would have been able to see the homes of fellow-Celts in larger settlements and on higher hills including Garn Fadryn, Garn Boduan and Tre'r Ceiri. Some experts believe it was the invading Romans who ended the occupation of these forts, whereas others maintain that they showed little interest in the land west of their major garrison at Segontium, Caernarfon.

Remains of other forts from the same period as Pen-y-gaer can be seen at Castell, in a dramatic spot overlooking the sea near Porth Ceiriad and at Nant-y-Castell on Mynydd Tir-y-Cwmwd, Llanbedrog. People in these coastal settlements would have been fishermen as well as farmers who grew corn and reared cattle, sheep and goats. It's

Garn Fadryn

Garn Boduan

A recreated Celtic village at the Museum of Welsh Life

A hut at Tre'r Ceiri

amazing to think that their language would have been Brythonic, an earlier form of the *Cymraeg* which is still spoken in the area today.

But there were people living in this part of Pen Llŷn for thousands of years before the Iron Age. At Trwyn Llech y Doll in Cilan and Bryn Parc, Llanbedrog you can see the remnants of cromlechi, or dolmens, burial sites from the Bronze Age period. There are better preserved ones in other parts of Llŷn, notably at Cefnamwlch near Tudweiliog and on the outskits of Y Ffôr. That any have survived is amazing: they are one or two thousand years older than the pyramids of Egypt.

In 1956, following a gorse fire on Mynydd Rhiw, a series of holes were noticed in the ground. That was how archaeologists came to discover the site of an important Stone Age axe factory. There were five round pits in a row about a hundred yards long, with rubble alongside containing rejected axes. The factory produced small axes for local use and larger ones for cutting trees in other areas. Some of the axes produced on Mynydd Rhiw have been discovered as far away as Gwent, which shows that there must have been an extensive commercial network operating at the time. Who says *Cymru* has no entrepreneurial tradition?

Fort at Pared Mawr

Bryn Parc cromlech

The Age of the Saints was one of the most significant periods in the history of Cymru. Its importance in shaping the country's character is demonstrated by the fact that we have around 650 place names beginning with 'Llan', usually followed by the name of a saint. 'Llan' originally meant an enclosure but evolved into a settlement gathered around a church. Places named after a saint were sometimes consecrated directly by the saint, and sometimes by his or her followers. The Christian tradition was strong in the Pen Llŷn area because of the importance of Ynys Enlli, the island of saints. Two pilgrimages to Enlli carried the same status as one to Rome.

Tudwal, who gave his name to the two islands off Abersoch, was a sixth century saint who was born in Cornwall and is also commemorated in Britanny. There is a tradition that he established a religious community on the larger of the two islands, which has the remains of a thirteenth century church. Both islands are now in private ownership, but there are boat trips around them from Abersoch.

The church at Llanengan, the centre of the large parish that contains Abersoch, has close ties with Enlli. Its patron saint, Engan or Einion, was one of the three founders of the monastery on the island. Much of the present building of St Einion's church, with its square tower, three bells and arched windows, dates from the end of the fifteenth century. The bells, a screen and an oak chest that used to house the church

Font at Llanengan

Llanengan church

ttreasures are thought to have come from the St Mary's monastery on Enlli. The chest was carved from a single piece of wood and originally had three locks with a key each given to the vicar and two church wardens. Even saints were not above temptation.

At the western end of the church a weekly school was held for a period at the end of the 18th century, with the help of one of Cymru's foremost educators. Griffith Jones, rector of Llanddowror near Carmarthen, is remembered for the circulating schools he set up in his own locality, where children and adults would attend school in one location for three months at a time and taught to read the Bible and the catechism before the church moved somewhere else. This made a huge contribution towards making the country literate. And at the other end of Wales it was Griffith Jones who paid the wages of a teacher who taught the scripture and general knowledge at the church in Llanengan.

The rector of Llanddowror may not have travelled quite as much as the Saints of previous ages, but his influence was just as far-reaching in his own land.

Llangian, Llanfihangel and Nanhoron

In the church cemetery at Llangian, a picturesque village nestling in the hills, there is a memorial stone dating from the 5th or 6th century bearing the Latin words *'Meli Medici Fili Martini Jacit'* – 'Here lies Meli the Doctor, Son of Martinus'. Who was Meli and what had he done to deserve this monument? We can only speculate that he was very highly respected, as this is the only tombstone from that period in Wales and England to specify that the person buried was a doctor by profession.

There is another interesting church at Llanfihangel Bachellaeth - the quietest place in Llŷn' according to Pwllheli-born poet Cynan. One reason for its quietness is that it's not the easiest place for strangers to find, on a maze of winding lanes somewhere between Nanhoron, Mynytho and Rhydyclafdy. The same remoteness is one reason why the church of St Mihangel ceased being a place of regular worship at the beginning of the twentieth century and has since been deconsecrated and sold to a private owner.

The present plain, rectangular building dates from the 17th century, and has a gallery with an external staircase added in 1847. Many of its artefacts have disappeared and a mounting stone on top of which the evangelist Howel Harris is said to have preached towards the end of the 17th century has been relocated outside the Calvinistic Methodist chapel at Rhydyclafdy.

Howel Harris, a native of Trefeca near Brecon, was the main leader of the Methodist Revival in Wales and his visits to Llŷn had an unexpected influence on the country's religious life. Harris started travelling on his missions in the company of Madam Sidney Griffith,

Llangian

 Howel Harris's mounting stone at Rhydyclafdy chapel

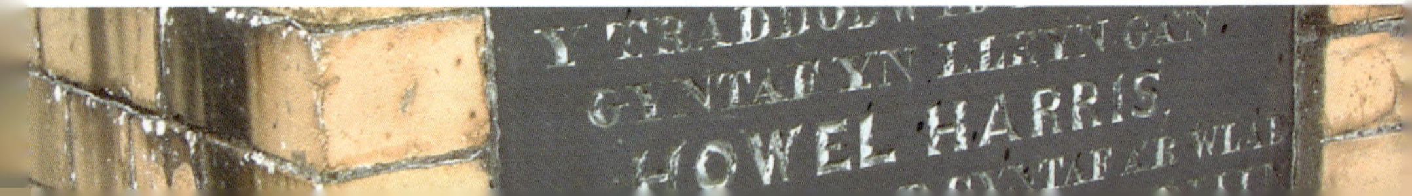

'Prophetess of the Methodist Revival', who was married to the drunken squire of Cefnamwlch. near Tudweiliog. There was much speculating about the nature of the relationship between her and Harris, which deepened an already developing rift within the Methodist Movement. In the midst of what would today be referred to as a scandal, Harris gave up his evangelizing.

At Nanhoron there is another place of worship immortalised in a poem by Cynan. Although its name, Capel Newydd, means new chapel it is the oldest nonconformist place of worship still standing in northern Wales. Described by Cynan as a small, whitewashed chapel in the far end of Llŷn, it was built in 1769 on the Nanhoron Estate and with the support of the Lady of the Manor, Catherine Edwards. Unusually for her class, she had deserted the Anglican faith and joined the Independent denomination because of the kindness shown to her by Nonconformists after her soldier husband died on a ship on his way home from war in the West Indies.

The building was declining rapidly until the 1950s, when local people came together to restore it to its original condition. Today it is in the care of conservation agency CADW.

And although the church of Llanfihangel Bachellaeth has also experienced decline, it is still an attraction for people who would never have heard of it were it not for Cynan.

Llanfihangel Bachellaeth

Capel Newydd

Gruffudd ap Cynan

In the days when it was easier to travel by sea than by land, natural coves such as Porth Ceiriad, Porth Neigwl and Bwlchtocyn became useful stations on the busy maritime highway along the western seaboard of Europe. With the Wicklow Hills clearly visible from Llŷn or a clear day, it is little wonder the Irish connection forms an important part of the area's heritage. Gruffudd ap Cynan, King of Gwynedd, epitomized that connection.

He was born in 1055 in Ireland, where his father was living in exile having been ousted from his Gwynedd throne by devious means. Gruffudd's mother was the daughter of a Dublin Scandinavian king. On his father's death the young Gruffudd came to Wales with a group of followers to try and regain his rightful heritage, but having won battles in Llŷn and Meirionnydd, he was defeated at Clynnog by Trahaearn, an impostor who had claimed his throne. The cause was not helped by animosity between Gruffudd's supporters in Llŷn and Scandinavians who had come over from Ireland to fight on his behalf. Gruffudd had to flee back to the land of his birth.

In 1081 he landed in Dyfed, and helped his friend, Rhys ap Tewdwr, to regain the throne of Deheubarth. But although his old adversary Talhaiarn was killed in battle, Gruffudd was betrayed by Meirion Goch, who lived in Castellmarch. He had invited Gruffudd to Rhug near Corwen to meet two Norman leaders, the Earls of Chester

A Norman castle stood on this rock at Abersoch

Porth Ceiriad

and Shrewsbury to discuss a peaceful settlement. The Normans had virtually conquered England in one battle in 1066, but found the mountainous and fractious Cymru more of a challenge. When Gruffudd and a band of friends arrived in Rhug the Normans cut the right thumbs of his followers before releasing them, and imprisoned Gruffudd in Chester. He escaped after 12 years and lived on the run. Eventually he made his way to from Aberdaron to Ireland with the help of monks from Ynys Enlli. .

He assembled a fleet of 23 ships and returned again to Cymru to confront Huw Flaidd, Earl of Chester. This time he got enthusiastic support from Llŷn ac Eifionydd and with his allies in Deheubarth kept the Romans at bay, inspiring one of the most unified and productive periods in the nation's history. The invaders were defeated and north and south-western Wales were rid of Normans for a whole generation.

Gruffudd was a man of culture as well as a soldier and a rebel. He is said to have introduced a new set of metrical forms for poetry and music, possibly influenced by the Irish soldiers who accompanied him in battle. In his final years he witnessed a cultural and political renaissance and a renewed sense of nationhood which persists to this day.

Mining

A tall chimney stack on a hill between Llanengan and Porth Neigwl is the most prominent reminder of an industry that no-one would have expected to see in a picturesque rural area. For centuries men toiled underground looking for lead, silver, copper, iron ore and manganese, as their masters' dreams of fortunes fluctuated and were often shattered.

There is a belief that the Romans were the first to exploit the mineral wealth of the area, but evidence of such activity is scarce. According to John Bennett and Robert Vernon, authors of *Metal Mines of Llanengan* (Gwydyr Mines Publications, 2003) the earliest record of mining is found in letters written in 1638 by Thomas Bushell, seeking permission to mine silver for a new royal mint he had set up in Aberystwyth castle. That venture was short-lived, and subsequent mining projects in Llanengan and Bwlchtocyn were sporadic and generally none too successful. One owner found the going so hard that he had to pay his men in potatoes instead of money! Another decided there was no substitute for experience and recruited tin workers from Cornwall to try and reverse his fortunes. A plaque commemorates Cornish Row, the now demolished houses where the incomers lived on Penrhyn Du. Pumping water from the mines was expensive, the geology challenging, the markets uncertain and relations with other mining companies such as those on Mynydd Parys in Anglesey awkward and uncertain. Despite all this the industry

Mining waste tips at Bwlchtocyn

The remains of the tower at Bwlchtocyn

kept expanding and employed 300 workers in it heyday in the 1870s.

A jetty was built at the foot of Penrhyn Du to load and unload ships, with a tramline from there to Llanengan. The bed of the tramline is still visible, and some of the company buildings form part of the Porth Tocyn Hotel.

As with all mining, it was not an easy occupation. Accidents were frequent, the most serious one occurring in 1885 when three workers at the Pant Gwyn works drowned after the shaft where they were working was flooded with water from an adjoining shaft. Safety inspectors' investigation showed that company bosses had miss-calculated the relative positions of the two shafts – instead of having 40 feet of earth between them at the level where the men were working, they were actually only 9 feet apart. John Hughes, William Ellis and Owen Jones paid with their lives, and the mine owner and his manager got away with a £20 fine.

Today most of the shafts have disappeared and only those familiar with the site can recognise other evidence of the activity. But the ventilation shaft was renovated at the end of the 1990s and stands as a proud monument to an exiting and unlikely chapter in the history of the parish of Llanengan.

The Madryn family and their church

The burial of Sir Love Jones Parry of Madryn in St Pedrog's church, Llanbedrog, happened in two stages. The squire himself witnessed the first occasion, when only his leg was buried. Doctors had amputated it following a mishap with a scythe. An anecdote circulating quite recently claimed that he had been knighted by default, having told Queen Victoria he had lost his leg 'in the field' and being rewarded for his war heroics. In fact he had been a two-legged knight for years before the accident. On his death in 1853 he was reunited with the missing limb.

On the wall of the church there is a plaque in honour of one of his ancestors, Love Jones Parry the First, who, according to the inscription, was "Universally lamented, because universally loved". Although the family is associated with Madryn, a mansion at the foot of Garn Fadryn, their original home was Cefn Llanfair, Llanbedrog. Their association with Eglwys Pedrog went back centuries: some of the family graves had been destroyed by Cromwell's soldiers.

The church's stained glass window was wrecked in the same attack, but the parishioners gathered the parts and hid them in a wooden chest. When the Madryn family built the present church in 1865 the parts that survived were put together again. A church screen was also salvaged and hidden on the beach until the conflict was over.

The most colourful member of the Madryn family was undoubtedly Thomas Love Duncome Jones Parry, son of the man who lost his leg, a playboy whose exploits

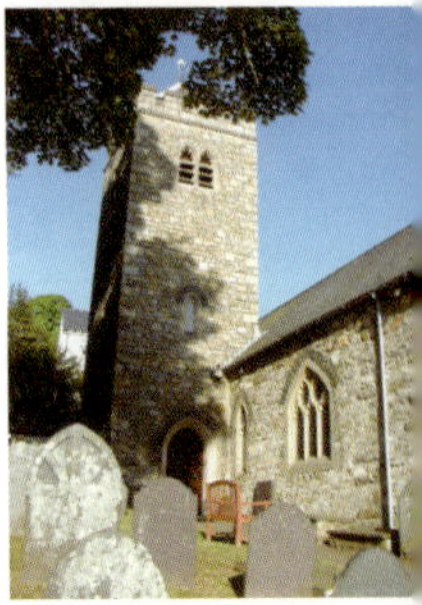

A part of Llanbedrog's screen

would have delighted today's tabloid journalists. In 1859 he was sentenced to death in Spain after trying to ride a horse over the border from Gibraltar and using his whip to attack the sentry who apprehended him. It was Queen Victoria's pleading that saved his life. He ventured into politics an won the Caernarfon seat for the Liberals in 1868. But the new MP was more interested in London's clubs and various racecourses than in the House of Commons. He only asked one question while he was there – during one debate he said he was not feeling well and asked if he could open a window.

His biggest adventure came in 1862 when he travelled to Argentina with Lewis Jones to pave the way for what became the Welsh colony established three years latger in Patagonia. It is doubtful if 'Parry Madryn' as he is still remembered by the Welsh-speaking Patagonians, ever set foot in that remote land, having sampled the delights of Buenos Aires' nightclubs.

And yet the landing place of the Mimosa, the ship that carried the first Welsh settlers, was christened Porth Madryn, and appears as Puerto Madryn on today's maps. It was there,ironically, that Argentinian prisoners of war landed on their way home from the Falkland or Malvinas Islands at the end of the 1982 conflict.

Today there is nothing left of the original Madryn in Llŷn. But another mansion built by the family is flourishing, not far from the family's graves in Llanbedrog.

Plas Glyn-y-Weddw

An art gallery, restaurant, book and record shop, education centre and several other things besides, it is little wonder that Plas Glyn-y-Weddw, Llanbedrog is one of the most popular tourist attractions in Llŷn. It was built in 1856 by Lady Elizabeth Love Jones Parry, mother of the prodigal son described in the last chapter. She was the widow who gave her name to the Plas and to a nearby pub (*Glyn* = glen, *gweddw* = widow). There is no record of her ever having slept in the mansion, although the house and gardens cost her £20,000. But a coach would transport her there every week from her home in Madryn.

In 1894 the house was sold to Solomon Andrews, a Cardiff-based entrepreneur who at the time was frantically reshaping parts of Pwllheli. Having built a hotel and substantial houses on the promenade there, he laid a tramline linking the town with Llanbedrog. The western terminal was opposite the entrance to Plas Glyn-y-Weddw, and the Plas became an integral part of his tourist plans. He opened an art gallery there, as well as a tearoom and dancehall, where visitors could enjoy themselves before catching the horse-drawn tram back to Pwllheli.

The tram came to a final stop when a severe storm destroyed the track in 1927. The Plas was sold in 1946 and declined rapidly until 1990 when it was bought by local artist Gwyneth ap Tomos and her husband Dafydd. They patiently renovated the building and reopened it as an art

gallery once more. It is now looked after by a trust, and attracts 20,000 visitors a year. Art exhibitions are rotated every five weeks or so. There are permanent exhibitions giving the history of the Love Parry and Andrews families, including a valuable collection of Nantgarw and Swansea porcelain leant by the descendants of Solomon Andrews.

The tearoom specialises in local produce, there are regular art courses and the Plas is becoming a popular venue for weddings. There is accommodation for people on residential courses, and evening courses are also provided.

For 50 years in the last century an imposing white statue looked down on Plas Glyn-y-Weddw and Llanbedrog from the top of Mynydd Tir Cwmwd. There were many tales about its alleged origin, but it was actually a ship's figurehead brought from Cardiff by Solomon Andrews. When it was destroyed by fire at the end of the 1970s, local artist and sculptor Simon Van der Put was commissioned to build a replacement. *'Y Dyn Haearn'* – 'Iron Man' – has just been renovated after years of heavy pounding by the weather.

But if the white statue is no longer there, there is still talk of a white lady in Llanbedrog. There are reports that Lady Love Jones Parry, who never stayed a night at Plas Glyn-y-Weddw during her life, still pays the occasional visit.

The 'Iron Man' on the cliff above Llanbedrog could be a metaphor for the iron that exists in the cultural identity of Llŷn which has survived centuries of pounding. A recent inspectors' report on Abersoch primary school, which educates three- to eight-year-olds before they move to another school at Sarn Bach, contained good and bad news for people concerned with the future of Cymraeg. Only 5% of the pupils lived in Welsh-speaking households. But every one had 'a good grasp of the language' by the time they left for Sarn Bach, and the way they mastered Cymraeg from an early age was 'one of the main successes of the school'.

This demonstrates the finely-balanced hopes and concerns about the effects of tourism, an industry that came to the area more than a hundred years ago but whose recent growth has increased both the economic prosperity and the cultural threat. As far back as the beginning of the twentieth century large houses were being built specifically for outsiders, some as holiday homes and others for families who had come to the area as tourists, liked what they saw and decided to stay.

For much of the century 'keeping visitors' became a way of life for many if not most local people. Letting your house for a couple of months in summer and moving your family to a shed or caravan was not an ideal lifestyle, but it brought some welcome extra cash towards bringing up the children in an area where well-paid jobs were in short supply. At the start of every year the business of 'letting' would become a main topic of conversation among the women, a couple of 'empty' weeks in July a

Abersoch school

matter for concern. When summer arrived the locals would watch out for the same familiar faces, as they would for migrating birds. Some tourists aroused extra curiosity. 'Have you seen the matches people yet?' 'No but I caught a glimpse of the whisky man the other day.' The owners of England's Glory and Haig's Whisky were said to be among the regular visitors.

Towards the end of the 1970s the change in the character of Abersoch, and other villages to a lesser extent, began to accelerate. Slack planning regulations led to large private housing estates not related to local needs. The prime example is Stad Cae Du, where nearly all the houses are in darkness throughout the winter months. Today most of the people living in Abersoch, including relative newcomers, are aware of the dangers of over-development. The huge increase in house prices is of concern to all except the sellers, and too many jetskis and similar devices could ruin the very qualities that attract people here.

The relationship between the native and incoming communities has been generally friendly. The sponsors of the village hall, described in the next chapter, were not alone in contributing generously to the life of the community. Many incomers are learning Cymraeg, and most want their children to do so. That is the most encouraging sign for the language spoken since the beginning os civilisation in Abersoch.

Llangian cottages

Beach huts at Llanbedrog

Halls

‘Winterbotham’ is not a common surname in Llŷn, but it’s a familiar one to those who frequent Abersoch village hall. Above the entrance there is a plaque informing us that the building was erected in 1914 by Mr and Mrs William H Winterbotham, Craig y Môr in memory of their son, Harold. Harold had been a missionary, and after contracting TB during his travels he joined his parents in Abersoch where he died in 1913.

The hall was not Sir William Winterbotham’s only favour to his adopted land. At around the same period smallholders in Cilan, led by Laura Jones, Bryn ’Rodyn, were in dispute with Francis Cooper Dunville Smythe, who had bought a cottage and some land there. Smythe tried to ban access to part of Mynydd Cilan, common land with a long traditiion of grazing rights. Pwllheli magistrates sided with the owner, but in a High Court appeal Sir William, one of the UK’s leading barristers, represented the farmers and won their case.

Through the years, Neuadd Abersoch has been a busy cultural and social centre and the home of a successful drama company. The building has been extended one part now houses a local history museum for a period every summer.

The people of nearby Mynytho did not need a rich benefactor to build their village hall. Having been given a plot of land by a farmer, they spent years raising money for the venture during the 1930s’

A view from Cilan

Abersoch village hall

Trwyn Cilan from Porth Neigwl

depression. Then they set about building it themselves, mostly through voluntary labour by unemployed people, and completed the task within six months which included the exceptionally hot summer of 1935. Neuadd Mynytho has been immortalised by a poem. At its official opening there were many longwinded speeches, and then a shy, bespectacled man stood up. Robert Williams Parry, one of *Cymru*'s best ever poets, read an englyn, a four-line stanza in strict metrical form, describing the labour of love that had turned a community's collective dream into a stone and timber reality.

Williams Parry's englyn, now displayed on a slate on the wall of the building, has become an icon and an inspiration for other communities involved in cooperative self-help. It can even be seen on the wall of a new Welsh language community centre and nursery school in Esquel at the foot the Andes, built through voluntary efforts in Patagonia and Cymru. It is fitting that the efforts of the working people of Mynytho, as well as the adventures of Love Jones Parry of Madryn, should be commemorated so far from their homeland.

Neuadd Mynytho

'the stones were built with love'

What the Butler saw

Sir William Jones, squire of Castellmarch in the 17th century, was fed up with his butler. But there was no way of getting rid of him. Whenever Sir William tried to dismiss him the disloyal servant would only laugh.

But Sir Williams had connections with local smugglers. He paid them money to snatch the butler, take him away on a ship and dump him on some shore so far away that he would never again set foot in Castellmarch.

But the plot went wrong. During his time on the ship the butler befriended the crew and made such an impression that they eventually made him captain. He used his new influence to exact revenge. So the smugglers once again visited Castellmarch, this time to snatch Sir William and introduce him to distant places. After his involuntary exile he was eventually freed and allowed to return to Castellmarch a chastened man.

That is one of several tales about smugglers and pirates that have entered the area's folklore. The coastline is dotted with coves and caves that were used to store wines, whisky, brandy and other delicacies that would find their way to villages like Llanbedrog by cover of night. But it was not the ordinary people who benefitted from the spoils, and the squire of Castellmarch was not the only nobleman engaged in dubious dealings. The families of Cefnamwlch and Bodfel were also heavily involved.

In 1536 four suspicious ships dropped anchor off Abersoch, and a stock of contraband corn and wheat had already made its way to local farms before commissioners from London arrived to investigate. It transpired that John Griffith, Cefnamwlch and his cousin John Wyn ap Hugh, Bodfel, had already been on board two of the ships having discussions with the captains who were notorious smugglers. The two squires claimed they had done this to fulfil their duties as justices of the peace. But it was then discovered that John Wyn had bought the bulk of the cargo and sold it to John ap Robert of Castellmarch. The secret was divulged by John Griffith, Cefnamwlch, who felt he had not had his fair share from the deal.

Part of the tradition, as in many coastal areas, was to lure ships on to the rocks by false signals, in order to plunder the cargo. A ballad by local poet Ieuan Llŷn, relates the gruesome story of how a French ship was wrecked at Porth Neigwl in 1629. Not content with the cargo, the thieves murdered the crew and cut off their fingers and ears in order to remove their jewellery. Two men, known as Siôn y Sarn and Hugh Tregeili, were put on trial and hanged for the offence.

Ships

A lime kiln at Pen Cei is one of the few surviving relics from the maritime activities that enlivened Abersoch before tourism took over. It belonged to the period when little sailing ships would anchor in the bay and the farmers' horses and carts would travel from a wide area to gather coal and lime or to deliver their oats and cheese and the occasional pig for transportation to the markets. The 'Crik of Aber Soigh' was on a list in 1542 of ports where ships were allowed to land. Many ships were built here as well, though not as many as in Pwllheli or Nefyn, and 'going to sea' was until recently a natural career option for many young men, including the second sons of farrmes where the eldest brother would stay at home to help his father.

But you did not have to become a sailor to sample the adventures of the sea. For several centuries ships came to seek shelter between Abersoch and Ynysoedd Tudwal, a much-needed haven known as St Tudwal's Roads. The nearby Sarn Badrig was the final resting place of many ships, and the treacherous sea at Porth Neigwl fully justified the English version of its name – Hell's Mouth. The worst tragedy happened at the end of the 19th century when 16 small ships from Porthmadog were trapped in the bay during a vicious storm that wrecked them all except one.

The most famous ship that came to grief in the Roads was the *Ann Pugh*, known as 'Fflat Huw Puw'. Its name was immortalised in a series of sea shanties by J.Glyn Davies based on the once-busy port of Porthdinllaen.

Old seamen cottages at Llanbedrog

One of the old Abersoch boats

Siop Talafon

It sank in a storm in 1858.

When an Italian ship carrying potatoes was wrecked in the Roads, the crew were given accommodation in Talafon, a well-known family shop in Abersoch. They showed their gratitude by leaving some of their cargo behind, and 'tatws bach Talafon' yielded crops that fed local families for years afterwards.

Abersoch lifeboat celebrated its centenary in 2004 – despite having been established in 1869! That's because the original station closed in 1931 but a new one opened at a different site in 1965, making a total of 100 years'service. During that period the volunteers were called out 679 times, saving 267 lives.

The lifeboat played an important part in the life of the community over the years. In the early part of the last century children would flock to watch their heroes having their weekly practice, and today the lifeboat's open day is one of the highlights of the summer. The 'centenary' coincided with the launch of a new boat, the Margaret Bench of Solihull, named after a lady who was a regular visitor to the area and left money for the lifeboat in her will.

The nature of the calls reflects the changes in sea traffic and in the character of Abersoch. For several decades the vast majority of calls involved ships in trouble in the Roads and adjoining areas. Nowadays speedboats, jetskis and swimmers account for most emergencies.

The lifeboat house

William's beach – everyone welcome

'At Abersoch, consisting of a few houses upon the edge of the St Tudwal's Road, vessels are occasionally built…' That was how the traveller Edmund Hyde-Hall described the scene at the beginning of the 19th century, as quoted in *Walks on the Llŷn Peninsula* by N.Burras and J.Stiff. Between the middle of the 18th and the middle of the 19th centuries 14 small ships were built at Abersoch. harbour. It was the 1880s, after the railway had arrived in Pwllheli, that saw the beginning of the transformation of Abersoch from a quiet fishing village to one that depended heavily on tourism.

At the heart of the new industry was 'Glan Môr William', the local name for the section of beach nearest the village. It was owned by William Williams of Bennar, the man who started its tourist development. It is part of a long bow of fine sandy beaches between Trwyn Cilan and Llanbedrog, bearing resonant names such as Traeth Marchros, Traeth Lleferin, Traeth Tywyn y Fach, Traeth Castellmarch and Glan Môr Gwaith. The Gwaith (*works*) in the latter refers to the quarrying on Mynydd Tir Cwmwd.

Gruffydd Parry, author of the classic travel book *Crwydro Llŷn ac Eifionydd*, attributes the explosion of tourism at Abersoch in the second half of the last century to a 'popularising of popularity'. Such was the transformation that there are now only two or three regular lobstermen maintaining the fishing tradition that was once the sole or main livelihood of many of the men folk. It is another sign of the times that a policeman on a jetski sometimes patrols the waters to keep marine traffic under control.

But for all the changes, some of the maritime traditions are alive and well. Foremost

Abersoch beach

An old Abersoch fisherman

Sailing at Abersoch

Traeth Tywyn y Fach

among these is the annual regatta on the second Saturday in August. It was started in the 1880s and became a highlight of the year even for non-sailors who flocked to Pen-y-Bennar to watch the races. Today's competitors arrive from near and far, and although it is organised by an independent committee of local people, the event fits into the busy season of activities at the South Caernarfon Yatch Club, which strives to promote Abersoch as one of the best sailing venues in Europe. The regatta is no longer a one-day affair, but part of a week's events which include crab-catching competitions, raft races, a mackerel race, athletics and even a sand castle competition. Some tourists arrange their summer holiday so as to coincide with this week.

Abersoch sailors have close connections with Ceinewydd, or New Quay, in Ceredigion. For years boats from Ceinewydd would sail to Abersoch to compete in the regatta. On their way home they would be joined in a race by boats from Pwllheli, who would then take part in the regatta at Ceinewydd. Although that custom no longer exists, there is still a lot of traffic cross Bae Ceredigion between the two villages.

Llanbedrog also used to have its regatta, and although that is no longer held this village can also be proud of its seafaring tradition. And Rob Humphreys, currently one of the world's foremost racing boat designers, is a son of Llanbedrog.

Festivals

If Llanfihangel Bachellaeth is the quietest place in Llŷn, the noisiest is probably Abersoch and district for two days every July. That's when the Wakestock festival is held, a crazy amalgam of wakeboarding and rock music, the largest of its kind in Europe according to the organisers. During the day competitors from all over the world show their skills at Abersoch beach and the Pwllheli marina, and at night much of the population of Llŷn, through choice or otherwise, can hear the boom of the bands and see the scanning of the searchlights at Penyberth. The event is said to attract 10,000 people on the Saturday and the same number on the Sunday. Most come from afar and camp at Penyberth, but many local youngsters are also drawn to this rare extravaganza on their doorstep.

A different kind of music brings thousands to the area at the beginning of June. The Abersoch Jazz Festival was only started in 2002 but has grown every year and now features around two dozen bands from all over the world. One of the year's highlights is the Saturday morning parade where five white stallions from a local riding school lead the bands through the streets of the village, a truly remarkable sight. Some of the bands and artistes are world famous, but less experienced local performers also have a platform. Bands featured so far have come from New Orleans, the

Surfing at Porth Neigwl

Netherlands, Norway, Denmark – and Blaenau Ffestiniog!

The whole of July and August is almost a continuous party in Abersoch, with its local, national, British and international sailing events, and various tournaments at the golf club. But the challenge now is to extend the tourist season, as an increasing number of hotels and restaurants stay open throughout the year. This is helped by the surfing festival organised every October by a local business, the West Coast Surf Shop. The 2004 event nearly had to be postponed because the sea was too quiet, but then there were just enough waves in Porth Ceiriad for some of the world's most talented surfers to display their skills. October is also the month of the Abersoch Gourmet Week, a new and popular festival that features dishes from several countries.

To kick off the season, a walking festival, Gŵyl Gerdded Llŷn is a popular weekend event in May. It's an opportunity to learn about the nature, archaeology and history of some of the remotest parts of the peninsula. There are experts to guide you along the pilgrims' way towards Enlli, to see some of the hidden places associated with smugglers and shipwrecks, or to visit the hill forts at Tre'r Ceiri, Garn Fadryn a Garn Boduan.

Glan Môr Gwaith

'Diversification' was to be the salvation of agriculture a few years ago, and Phil and Meinir Roberts of Tanrallt, Llangian, took up the challenge. As a result you can now visit the farm to learn the brand new skill of piloting a hovercraft over their fields, either for pleasure or to gain Hovercraft Club of Great Britain qualifications. It's open throughout the year, offers self-catering accommodation at the Sgubor Unnos, and has a site for tents and caravans.

If you prefer a more conventional challenge, officers of Clwb Golff Abersoch claim with some justification that there is no better golf course in north western Wales. It was designed in 1908 as a nine-hole course, which has since been extended to 18. If your time is short you can always use Golff Llŷn, a nine-hole course and driving range at Penyberth. There are many riding and pony trekking centres in the area, and a triaining school for archery and clay-pigeon shooting at Llanbedrog. On the Caernarfon side of Pwllheli the go-karting and tenpin bowling centre at Glasfryn is becoming very popular.

Nowhere in Llŷn has a better selection of restaurants, hotels and pubs. You can taste Indian, Mexican, Italian and Welsh food without venturing beyond Abersoch and Llanbedrog.

And you don't have to be a sailor, swimmer or surfer to enjoy the sea. The regular boat trips from Abersoch round Ynysoedd Tudwal provide a good chance of seeing the occasional seal or dolphin, or observing some of the rare birds nesting on the island.

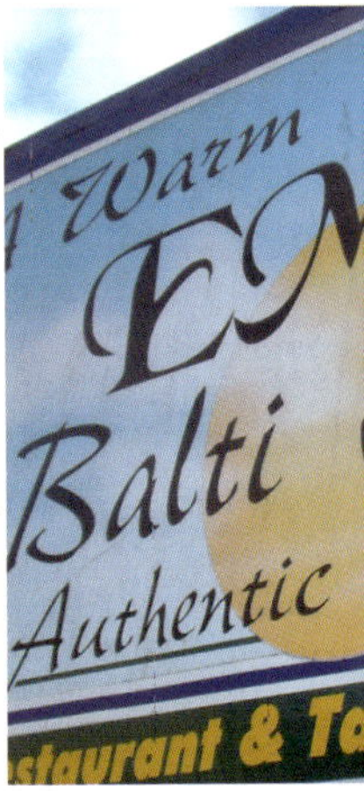

Foel Felin Wynt, Mynytho

Golf centre at Penyberth

Porth Ceiriad

And this brings us back to the beginning. For all the human activities that enliven the ardal, there is no doubt that its biggest charm is its natural beauty and sense of timelessness. Much of Pen Llŷn was designated an Area of Outstanding Natural Beauty in 1957, only the second place in the UK to be given that status. The landscape, with its green fields, high hedges and heather-clad hills create a unique atmosphere. And so do the coves, rocks and cliffs within Llŷn Coastal Heritage, a designation created by the Countryside Commission in 1974 to protect its natural heritage. Its logo shows the red-legged crow, a rare bird which nests on Trwyn Cilan and in other places around the Llŷn coast. It can be called a Celtic bird, as its other habitats include the Isle of Man, western Scotland and parts of Ireland and Britanny.

Whereas most people would prefer to do their rambling in sunshine, watching the waves in Porth Ceiriad on a stormy day can also be a mesmerising experience. There are useful books to help you interpret the past, including *Walks on the Llŷn Peninsula (Part 1, South and West)* by N.Burras and J.Stiff, and *Llŷn Peninsula Coastal Walks* by Richard A.R.Quine. *Llŷn* by Elfed Gruffydd is available in both languages, and for those who can read Cymraeg, *Ar Hyd Ben 'Rallt* by the same author is a thorough collection of place names and information. Gruffudd Parry's *Crwydro Llŷn ac Eifionydd* is enough reason in itself to learn the language!

LLANBEDROG
B4415
B4413
B4413
3
1
Mynydd
Tir-y-cwmwd
Mynytho
A499
Trwyn
Llanbedrog
Lan-Môr-Gwaith
2
Llangian
Traeth
Tywyn y Fach
ABERSOCH
Traeth
Abersoch
Afon Soch
Llanengan
PORTH NEIGWL
Ynysoedd
Tudwal
Bwlchtocyn
1 Plas Glyn-y-Weddw
2 Castellmarch
3 Old windmill, Mynytho
4 Fort at Porth Ceiriad
5 Cromlech, Mynydd Cilan
4
Porth Ceiriad
5
Trwyn
Cilan
MÔN
Llandudno
Conwy
Bangor
Caernarfon
Betws-y-coed
Pwllheli
Abersoch
ERYRI